# Is There SEX After RETIREMENT?

### Written by **Herbert I. Kavet & Toni Goffe**
### Illustrated by **Martin Riskin**
### Layout by **Coffey Cup Productions**

©1996 by **Boston America Corp.**

No portion of this book may be reproduced - mechanically, electronically, or by any other means including photocopying - without the permission of the publisher.

30 29 28 27 26 25 24 23 22 21 20 19 18 17 16 15 14 13 12 11 10 9 8 7 6 5 4 3 2

**Boston America Corp.**
125 Walnut Street, Watertown, MA 02172   617-923-1111   Fax: 617-923-8839

"Don't give me that 'I have to be at work tomorrow'."

"Now that we're retired we think we'll have time for group sex."

"You knew exactly what I meant by 'menage a trois'."

"I don't know either. Maybe he's from the mutual fund."

"Oh, we thought Sunny Acres was a retirement community."

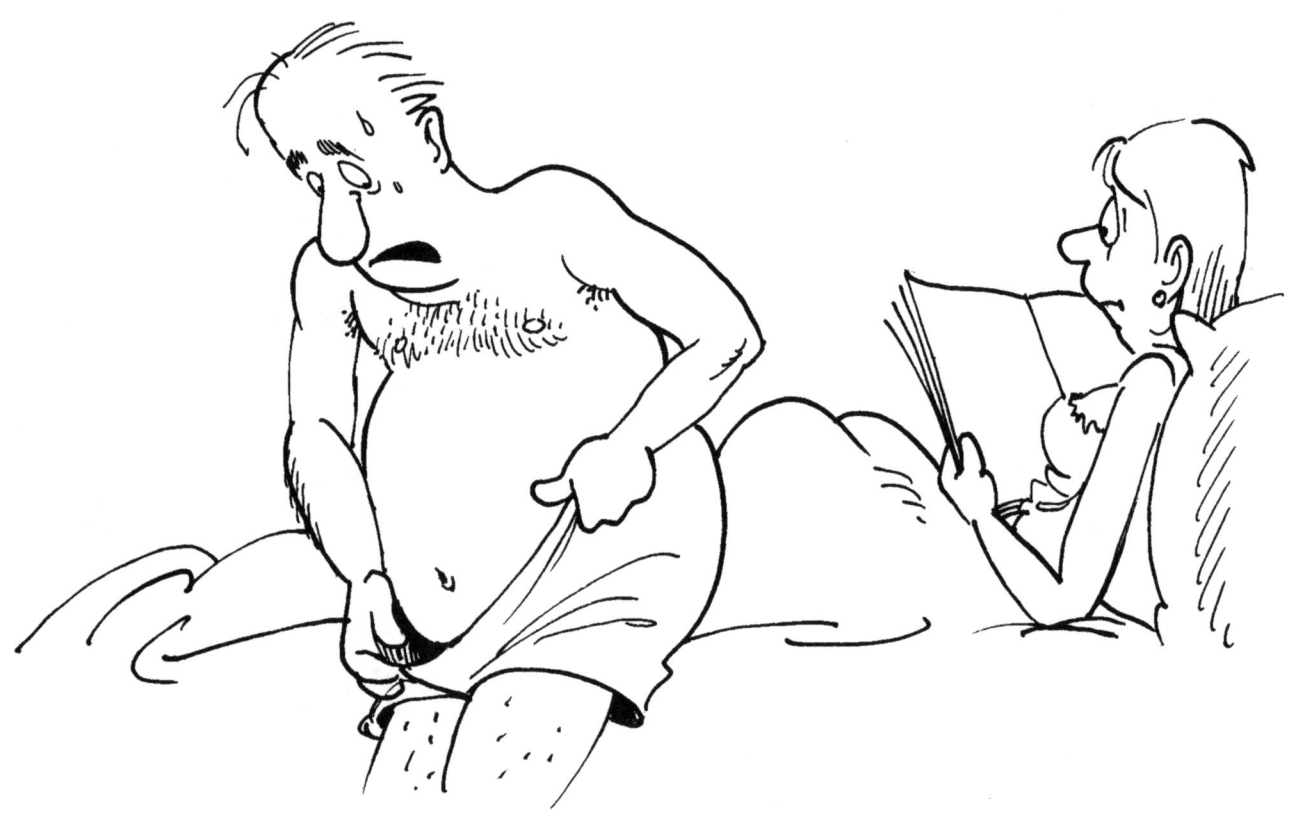
"Turning gray down there doesn't mean a thing."

"I suppose you're rushing for the early bird special so we can have a real long session of love and romance tonight."

"You used to get up in the middle of the night for me."

"Since we got Dad on line we can't tear him away from the computer."

"I don't know if he just forgets to zipper his fly or thinks it looks sexy."

"So, I've a stiff neck. You don't see me bragging about it all day."

"For God sake Mildred I won't take advantage of you if you get drunk, we've been married 30 years."

"Your exercise program definitely isn't improving our sex life."

"Charlie's been deeply disturbed since he retired."

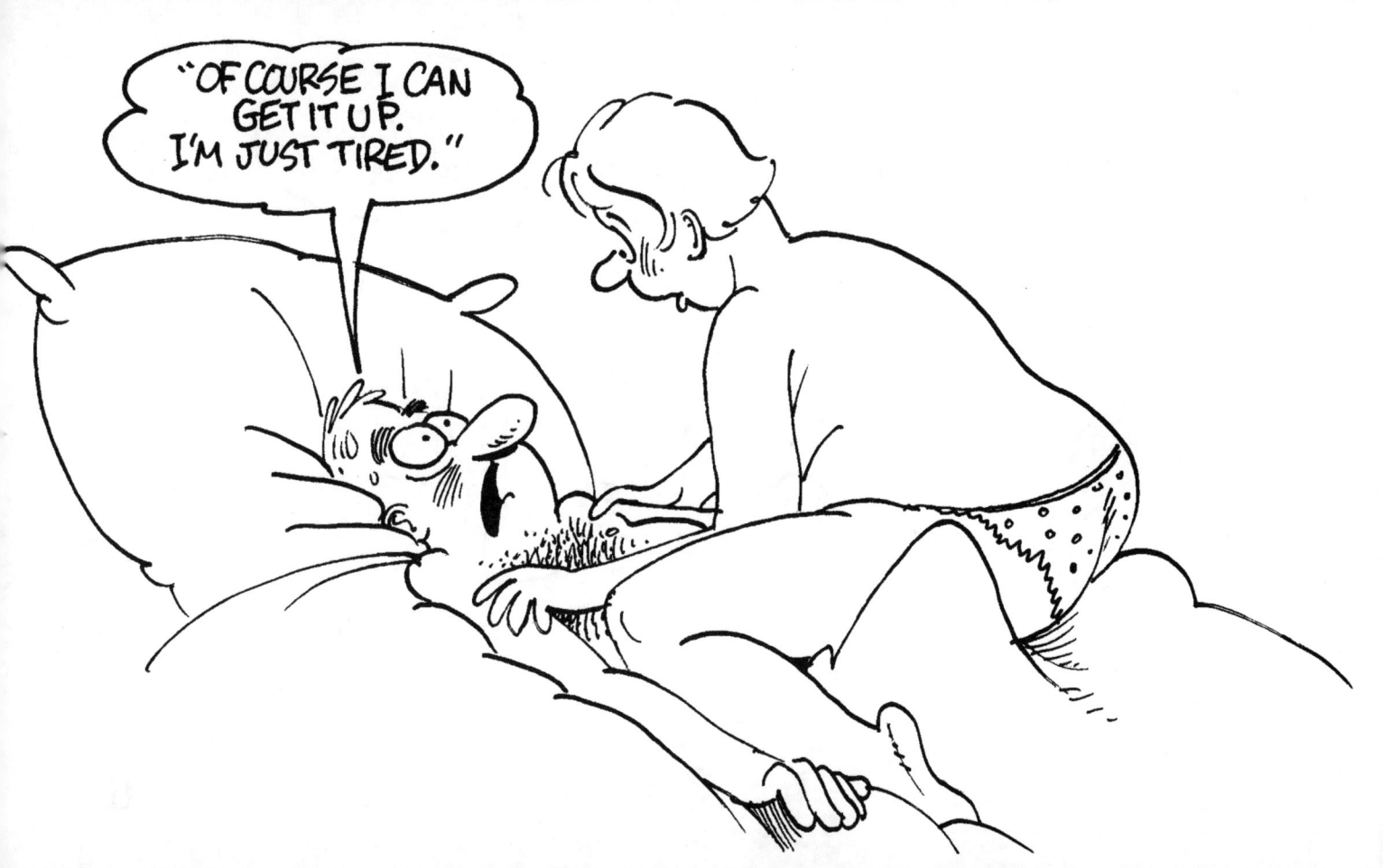

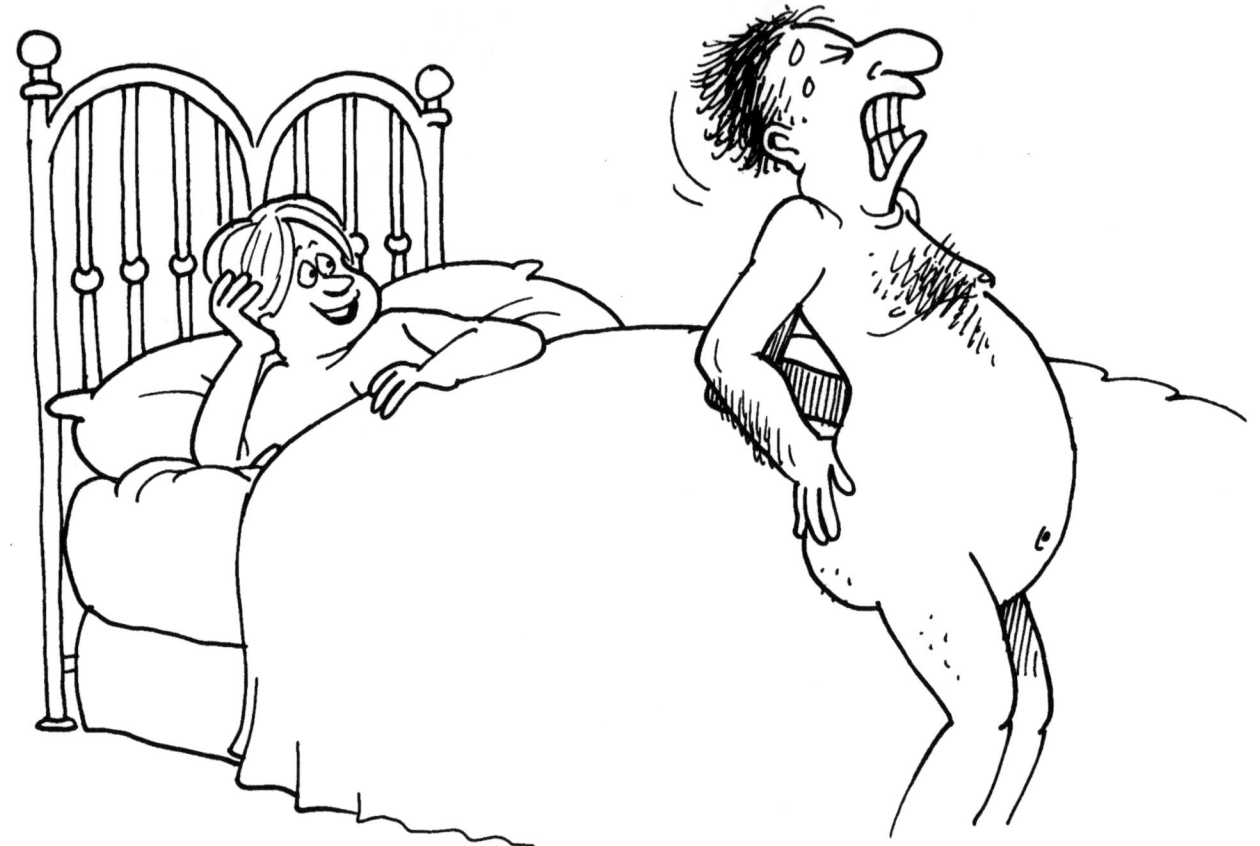

"Well if your back hurts you shouldn't do it."

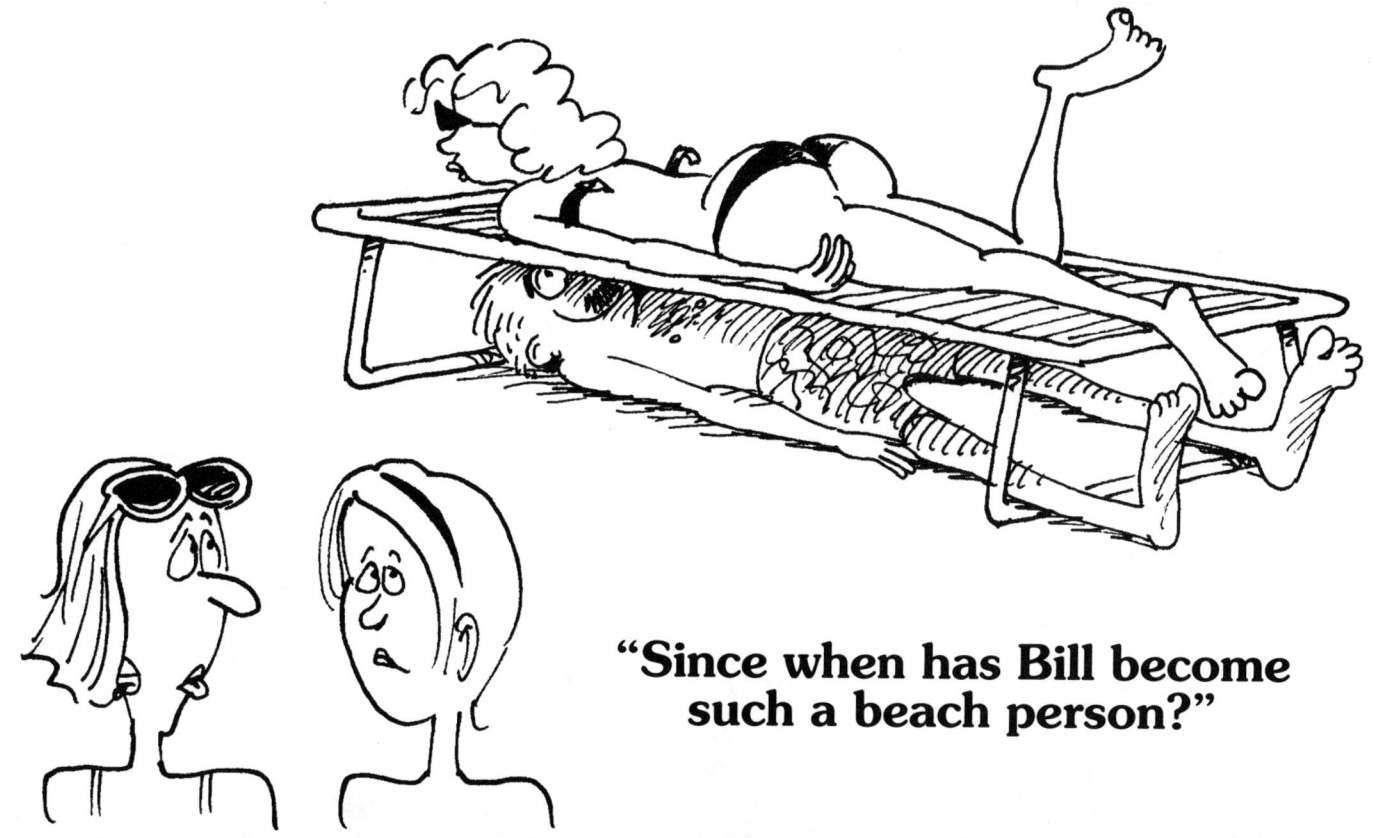

"If he were rigid I wouldn't be frigid."

"I'm not sure Mr. William's is ready for Retirement Acres."

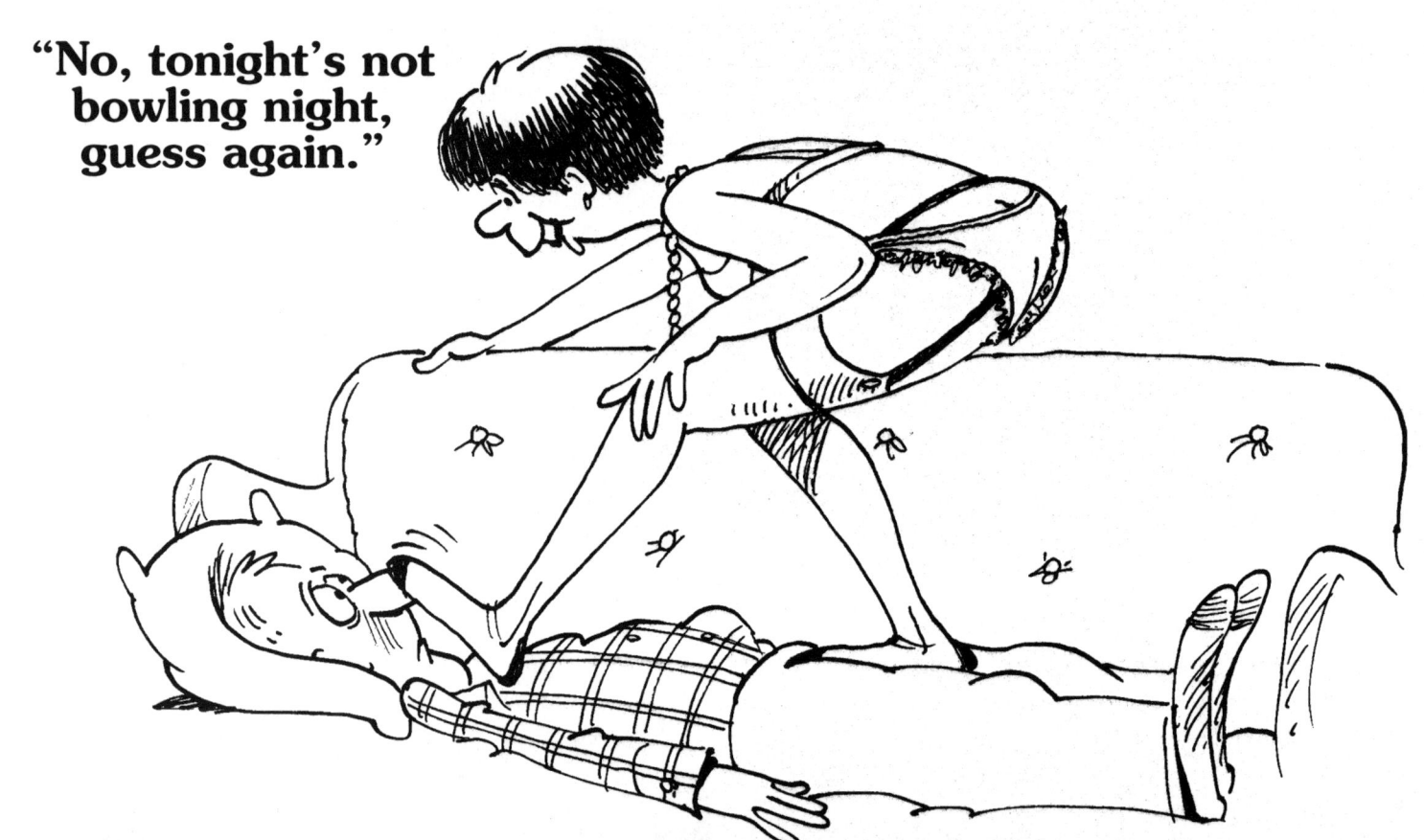

"Well, my kids never call for money at times like this."

"Bless You!"

"I don't think you understand what's meant by wife swapping Mr. Hargraves."

"It says retired couples should do it at least once a week."

"Aha, setting me up for the big seduction tonight I see."

"So I said, 'you're retired now, find a hobby, find a pastime'."

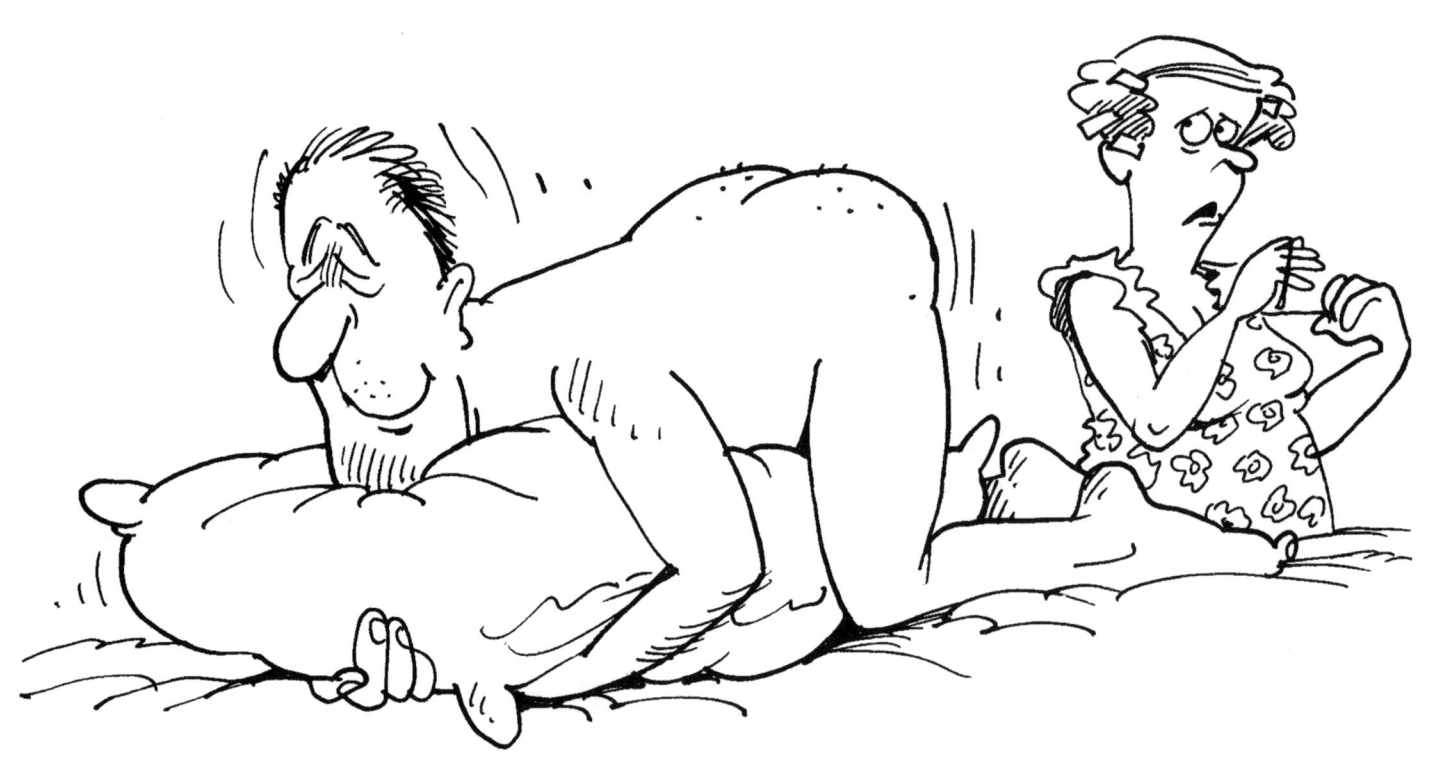

"Phillip, you've left your glasses downstairs."

"This may have been fun in high school but it's not so great when you're retired."

"Lets go shoot some dope, get plastered, watch some porn tapes then swing till dawn."

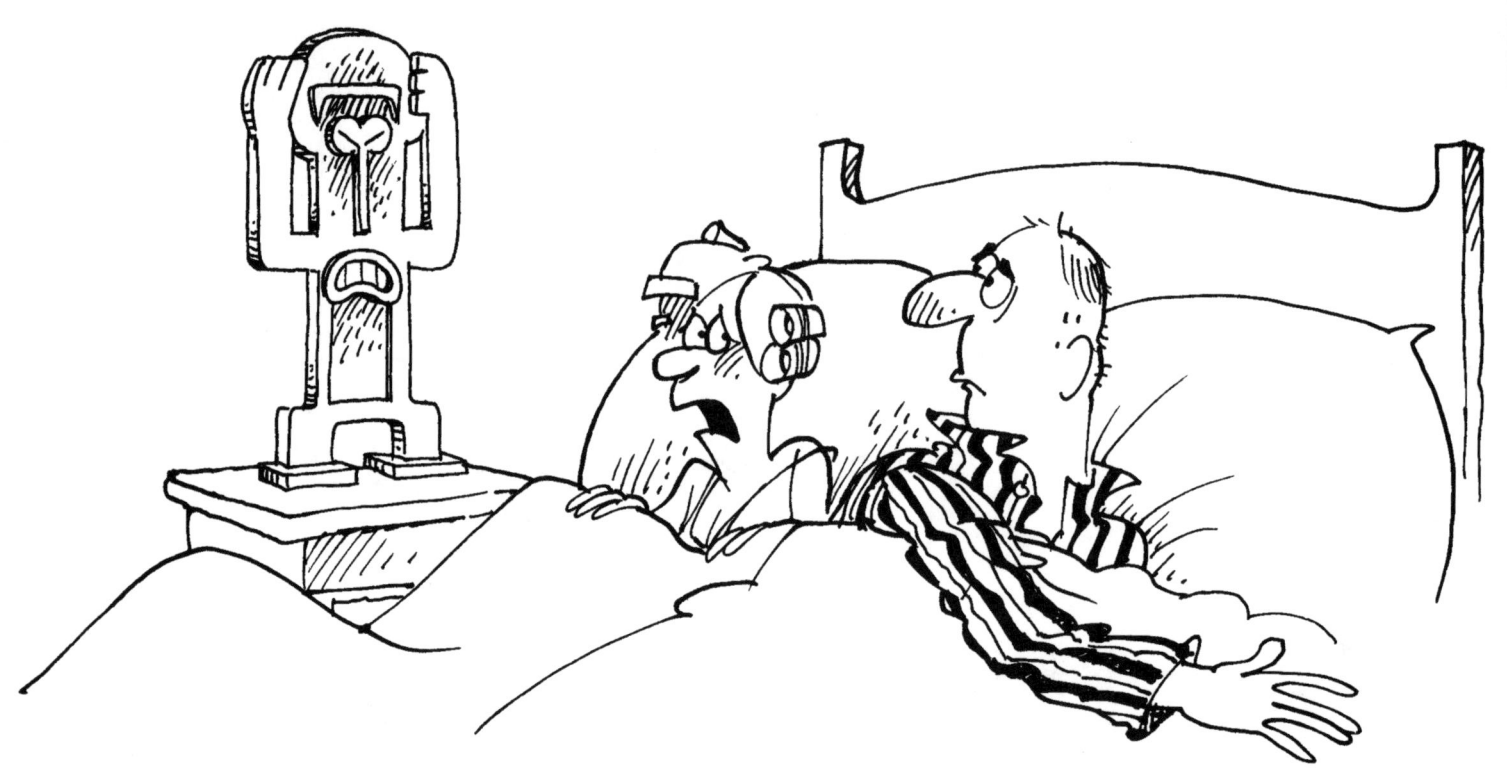
"It's the Patron Saint of headaches if you must know."

"Wow, that was the most erotic scene I've ever seen."

"I'm not sure the McDougals are ready for Quiet Acres Retirement Park."

"For Pete's sake, will you put that thing down."

# OTHER GREAT BOOKS BY BOSTON AMERICA

The fine, cultivated stores carrying our books really get ticked if you buy directly from the publisher so if you can, please patronize your local store and let them make a buck. If, however, the fools don't carry a particular title, you can order them from us for $7, postpaid. Credit cards accepted for orders of 4 or more books.

**#2400 How To Have Sex On Your Birthday**
Finding a partner, special birthday sex positions, kinky sex and much more

**#2403 The Good Bonking Guide**
Bonking is a very useful British term for "you know what" and this book covers bonking in the dark, bonking all night long, improving your bonking and everything else you might want to know.

**#2419 Cucumbers Are Better Than Men Because...**
Cucumbers never go soft in a second, aren't afraid of commitment and never criticize.

**#2423 Is There Sex After 40**
It says normal couples do it at least once a week, you get the urge but can't remember what for and "if he was frigid I wouldn't be frigid".

**#2424 Is There Sex After 50**
Swapping him for two 25 year olds, being into gardening, wine making and group sex and liking it better when the bulge was in his trousers.

**#2430 Is There Sex After 30**
Being too tired to get it up, thinking kinky is leaving the lights on and remembering when you could do it 3 times a night.

**#2432 Big Weenies**
Big weenies and small weenies and all their names and how to find big weenies in a strange town and how to rate them.

**#2434 Sex and Marriage**
Wives wanting foreplay and romance and husbands wanting to be allowed to go to sleep right after. Techniques for improving your wife or husband or ignoring them.

**#2438 Dog Farts**
Dogs get blames for lots of farts they don't do but this book gives all the real ones like the sleeping dog fart and the living room fart.

**#2446 The PMS Book**
This book covers all the problems from irritability to clumsiness to chocolate craving to backaches in a funny and sympathetic manner.

**#2450 How To Pick Up Girls**
This book holds the keys to understanding women and teaches never fail lines plus places to meet shy, drunk weird and even naked girls

**#2451 How To Pick Up Guys**
How to get them to grovel at your feet and how to spot the losers and how to get rid of them after sex.

**#2453 Beginners Sex Manual**
Covers basics such as how to tell if you're a virgin and good things to say before and after sex.

**#2455 Unspeakably Rotten Cartoons**
Words cannot describe this totally tasteless and crass collection of cartoons that are guaranteed to offend and make you laugh.

**#2457 Hooters**
This is a photo book of the latest lingo for boobs and bosoms and bulging breasts.

**#2458 Adult Connect The Dots**
If you can count and use a pencil at the same time you too can be a pornographer.

**#2463 Butts and Buns**
These photos take a racy, rear view at women's tushes, beautiful buns and delicate derrieres

**#2465 Do It Yourself Guide To Safe Sex**
Well if you do it yourself you can get it right the first time and never catch any nasty diseases

**#2466 Guide To Intimate Apparel**
Photos and purposes of all the lacy lingerie and unmentionables from bloomers to garters to wedgies.

**#2469 Hunks**
A list of all the popular men's names and how they compare in bed and boardroom and physical sizes,

**#2470 How To Find A Man And Get Married In 30 Days**
Reserve the hall first and then learn ways and places to meet men, how to use sex and how to get rid of your mistakes,

**#2471 Student Guide To Farting**
The roommate fart, the math teacher fart, the lunch lady fart. This book covers them all.

**#2472 Party Games For 30 Year Olds**
New racy games and lists of old favorites. This book has them all and will keep a party of 30 year olds going all night.

**#2473 Party Games For 40 Year Olds**
Similar to the 30 year old book with perhaps more emphasis on sex rather than drinking.

**#2474 Party Games For 50 Year Olds**
Just like the 30 and 40 year old games but this book gives instruction on keeping the players awake after 10 PM

**#2501 Cowards Guide To Body Piercing**
Cartoons and explanations of all the good and horrible places you can put holes in yourself.

**#2502 Toilet Tips**
Urinal etiquette and handling warm toilet seats or doors with lousy locks or smells that are not your own. A must for anyone that uses toilets.

**#2503 Kinky World Records**
Like the world's hairiest armpits or thickest condom or shortest male organ or longest time to take off a bra. Hey, you could set your own records.

**#2504 Pregnant Woman's Guide To Farting**
The Claustrophobia Fart and the Waiting Room Fart and the Naming the Baby Fart and the Constipation Fart are just a few.

**BOSTON AMERICA C★O★R★P**

125 Walnut Street, Watertown, MA 02172 (617) 923-1111  FAX: (617) 923-